D1709427

SADDLE UP!

Thoroughbred Horses

by Rachel Grack

BLASTOFF!
READERS
2

BELLWETHER MEDIA • MINNEAPOLIS, MN

Blastoff! Readers are carefully developed by literacy experts to build reading stamina and move students toward fluency by combining standards-based content with developmentally appropriate text.

Level 1 provides the most support through repetition of high-frequency words, light text, predictable sentence patterns, and strong visual support.

Level 2 offers early readers a bit more challenge through varied sentences, increased text load, and text-supportive special features.

Level 3 advances early-fluent readers toward fluency through increased text load, less reliance on photos, advancing concepts, longer sentences, and more complex special features.

★ **Blastoff! Universe**

Reading Level

Grade
K

Grades
1–3

Grade
4

This edition first published in 2021 by Bellwether Media, Inc.

No part of this publication may be reproduced in whole or in part without written permission of the publisher. For information regarding permission, write to Bellwether Media, Inc., Attention: Permissions Department, 6012 Blue Circle Drive, Minnetonka, MN 55343.

Library of Congress Cataloging-in-Publication Data

Names: Koestler-Grack, Rachel A., 1973- author.
Title: Thoroughbred horses / by Rachel Grack.
Description: Minneapolis, MN : Bellwether Media, Inc., 2021. | Series: Blastoff! readers: saddle up! | Includes bibliographical references and index. | Audience: Ages 5-8 | Audience: Grades K-1 | Summary: "Relevant images match informative text in this introduction to Thoroughbred horses. Intended for students in kindergarten through third grade"– Provided by publisher.
Identifiers: LCCN 2019054264 (print) | LCCN 2019054265 (ebook) | ISBN 9781644872369 (library binding) | ISBN 9781618919946 (ebook)
Subjects: LCSH: Thoroughbred horse–Juvenile literature.
Classification: LCC SF293.T5 K64 2021 (print) | LCC SF293.T5 (ebook) | DDC 636.1/32–dc23
LC record available at https://lccn.loc.gov/2019054264
LC ebook record available at https://lccn.loc.gov/2019054265

Editor: Elizabeth Neuenfeldt   Designer: Andrea Schneider

Printed in the United States of America, North Mankato, MN.

Table of **Contents**

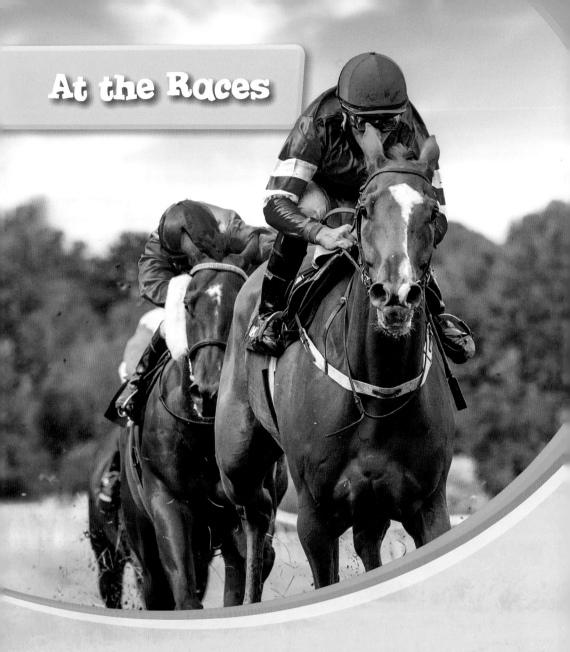

Thoroughbred horses are best known for racing.

They are the fastest horse **breed**. They can run over 40 miles (64 kilometers) per hour!

Racing Bodies

Thoroughbreds stand between 15 and 17 **hands** high.

They have wide and deep chests. This gives them more room to breathe while they run!

6

SIZE OF A THOROUGHBRED HORSE

15 to 17 hands

12 hands

20 hands

10 hands

0 hands

one hand = 4 inches (10 centimeters)

Thoroughbreds have **muscular** bodies. They stand on long, strong legs.

These sturdy horses weigh around 1,000 pounds (450 kilograms)!

Many Thoroughbreds have **bay**, black, or gray **coats**.

COAT COLORS

bay

black

gray

Most have white markings
on their faces and legs.

Thoroughbred Beginnings

Arabian stallion

Thoroughbreds started in England around the late 1600s.

Three Arabian **stallions** were **bred** with English **mares**. They made strong, fast horses.

England

N
W E
S

England

In the 1700s, people
wanted the best race horses.
Thoroughbreds were
the fastest and strongest.

THOROUGHBRED HORSE TIMELINE

LATE 1600S
Thoroughbreds
are created

1700S
More people
breed
Thoroughbreds

1730
Thoroughbreds
come to America

Many people liked them!
In 1730, Thoroughbreds
came to America.

Thoroughbreds have a lot of **energy**. But they can get **overwhelmed**.

These horses work best with skilled riders.

jump race

Thoroughbreds are quick on the racetrack. Many run in flat or **jump races**.

Their speed also makes these horses great in **show jumping**!

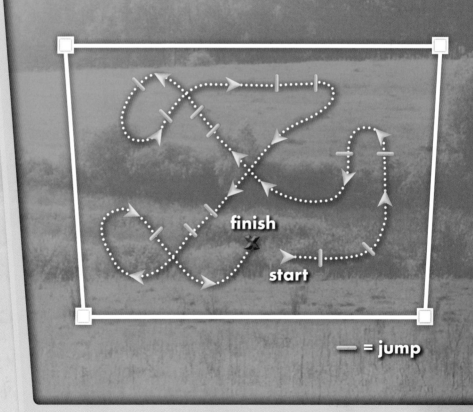

HORSING AROUND
SHOW JUMPING COURSE

finish

start

— = jump

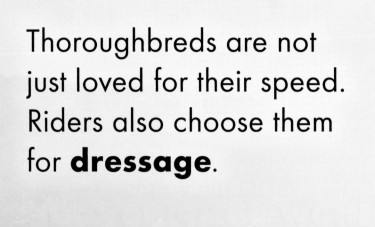

Thoroughbreds are not just loved for their speed. Riders also choose them for **dressage**.

dressage

These horses **thrill** crowds on and off the racetrack!

Glossary

bay—a coat color with a reddish-brown body and a black mane, ears, and tail

bred—mated with other horses to make horses with certain qualities

breed—a certain type of a horse

coats—the hair or fur covering some animals

dressage—a horse show event judged on movement, balance, and the ability to follow directions

energy—the power to move and do things

hands—the units used to measure the height of a horse; one hand is equal to 4 inches (10 centimeters).

jump races—races in which horses must go over different kinds of jumps

mares—female horses

muscular—related to large and strong muscles; muscles help animals and humans move.

overwhelmed—completely overpowered by thoughts and feelings

show jumping—the sport of riding horses one at a time over different jumps as quickly and skillfully as possible; it is also called jumping.

stallions—male horses

thrill—a strong feeling of happiness

To Learn More

AT THE LIBRARY

Diedrich, John. *Thoroughbred Horses*. North Mankato, Minn.: Capstone Press, 2018.

Meister, Cari. *Thoroughbred Horses*. Mankato, Minn.: Amicus, 2019.

Noll, Elizabeth. *Thoroughbred Horses*. Mankato, Minn.: Black Rabbit Books, 2019.

ON THE WEB

FACTSURFER

Factsurfer.com gives you a safe, fun way to find more information.

1. Go to www.factsurfer.com.

2. Enter "Thoroughbred horses" into the search box and click 🔍.

3. Select your book cover to see a list of related content.

Index

The images in this book are reproduced through the courtesy of; jacotakepics, front cover (horse); Vova
Shevchuk, pp. 2, 3, 23 (horseshoes); Sara Julin Ingelmark, pp. 4-5; Mark J. Barrett/ Alamy, pp. 5, 6-7, 16
(inset); Barry Fowler, p. 6 (inset); ashkabe, pp. 8-9; Juniors Bildarchiv GmbH/ Alamy, pp. 9, 10 (black); pirita,
p. 10 (bay); Sergey Nazarov/ Alamy, p. 10 (gray); Grigorita Ko, pp. 10-11; Rolf Kopfle/ Alamy, pp. 12-13;
PA Images/ Alamy, pp. 14-15; TeodorLazarev, pp. 16-17; MediaWorldImages/ Alamy, pp. 18-19; Lauren
Nicole H, p. 20; Gaertner/ Alamy, pp. 20-21.